BOOKS BY PHILIP LEVINE

POETRY

THE MERCY 1999
UNSELECTED POEMS 1997
THE SIMPLE TRUTH 1994
WHAT WORK IS 1991
NEW SELECTED POEMS 1991
A WALK WITH TOM JEFFERSON 1988
SWEET WILL 1985
SELECTED POEMS 1984
ONE FOR THE ROSE 1981
7 YEARS FROM SOMEWHERE 1979
ASHES: POEMS NEW AND OLD 1979
THE NAMES OF THE LOST 1976
1933 1974
THEY FEED THEY LION 1972
RED DUST 1971
PILI'S WALL 1971
NOT THIS PIG 1968
ON THE EDGE 1963

ESSAYS

THE BREAD OF TIME 1994

TRANSLATIONS

OFF THE MAP: SELECTED POEMS OF GLORIA FUERTES, EDITED AND TRANSLATED WITH ADA LONG 1984

TARUMBA: THE SELECTED POEMS OF JAIME SABINES, EDITED AND TRANSLATED WITH ERNESTO TREJO 1979

INTERVIEWS

DON'T ASK 1981

THEY FEED THEY LION

THE NAMES OF THE LOST

PHILIP LEVINE

THEY FEED THEY LION

THE NAMES OF THE LOST

NEW YORK ALFRED A. KNOPF

1999

THIS IS A BORZOI BOOK
PUBLISHED BY ALFRED A. KNOPF, INC.

Published in the United States by Alfred A. Knopf, Inc., New York, and simultaneously in Canada by Random House of Canada, Limited, Toronto. Distributed by Random House, Inc., New York.

www.randomhouse.com

Originally published as two separate volumes by Atheneum, New York, in 1972 and 1976.

The Names of the Lost was originally published in a limited edition by The Windhover Press of The University of Iowa.

Library of Congress Cataloging-in-Publication Data
Levine, Philip
They feed they lion: &, The names of the lost / Philip Levine.—
1st Knopf ed.
p. cm.
ISBN 0-375-70629-1 (alk. paper)
I. Levine, Philip. Names of the lost. II. Title.
III. Title: They feed they lion : &, The names of the lost.
IV. Title: Names of the lost.
PS3562.E9A6 1999
811'.54—dc21 99-10987
CIP

Manufactured in the United States of America
First Knopf Edition

CONTENTS

THEY FEED THEY LION

THE NAMES OF THE LOST

THEY FEED THEY LION

For those who helped me,
especially Fran,
my Lion, my Thistle, my Tree

RENAMING THE KINGS

River of green stone,
in August '62 I stuck my head in
your lap one mile south of Piedra
where you fall suddenly away
from the highway. 107
in the valley and me
going dizzy, stopped the bike
and stumbled down
over the flat, patient stone, leaned out,
and then you in my eyes,
green tatters of memory, glimpses
of my own blood flashing
like fish, the grasses
dancing calmly, one silver point
like the charmed eye of an eel.
Five hours later I wakened
with the first darkness flowing
from the river bottom
through me to stone, to
the yellow land grasses and storming
the lower branches of the eucalyptus.
I could feel the water
draining from my blood and the stone
going out—the twin bushes of the lungs
held themselves seriously
like people about to take fire,
and when the first minnows startled
I rose into the sky. We
gathered every last tendril
of blue into our breath.

I named the stone John
after my mysterious second born.
High in its banks, slashed with silver,
riding the jagged blade of heaven
down to earth, the river shouts its name.

THE SPACE WE LIVE

I

Light shrugs at the last dreams
of cops and whores. The three cold stacks
above the tire factory climb
the dawn. An old man, home from work,
sits on the bed, unlacing.
How small the space a man lives,
elbows on guard, the fingers
curled, the head tucked.

As a child I lived cupboards, drawers,
tiny hutches of straw and wax,
narrow fluted corridors
of the ear. At night I would spread
my arms and legs under the fresh sheets
and laugh to hear the first sly growls
of watch dog, the cluck of hen
in the silvery yards where mother moon waited.

II

The stained muzzle, the tail's
nervous quivering as though
an unfelt wind stirred, the fox
floats in the heavy smell
of its living,
and the singed blades of grass
spring upward after the passing.

Crow lives the horizon of squat olives,
approves of everything, outlasts
the barn mice searching the garbage
for their death, coyote
calls at the edge of light
until the dawn blooms slowly
from the elm leaves, and nothing
moves and nothing lives
for that one space before the word is flesh.

THE CUTTING EDGE

Even the spring water
couldn't numb the slash
of that green rock
covered with river lace.
Slowly the blood spread
from under the flap of skin
that winked open; deep in
my foot, for a second, I saw
something holding back,
and I sat down in the water
up to my waist in water,
my pockets filling with it.
I squeezed the green rock,
pressed it to my cheeks,
to my eyelids. I did not
want to be sick or faint
with children looking on,
so I held to the edge of the stone
until I came back.

That was a year ago.
I threw the stone away
as though I could banish it
from creation; I threw
it into the dry reeds,
where it could do no harm,
and dragged myself bleeding
up the hillside and drove home.

I forgot the stone
drying among burned reeds
in October; I forgot
how cold this place got
when the winds came down the pass,
and how, after the late rains,
the first pale ice-plants dot

the slopes like embroidery,
then larkspur, myrtle, and the great,
bellowing, horned blooms
that bring summer on.

Huddling to where it fell,
like a stunned animal,
the stone stayed. I kneel
to it and see how dust
has caked over half of it
like a protruding lip
or a scab on no cut
but on a cutting edge.
It comes away from the ground
easily, and the dry dirt
crumbles, and it's the same.
In the river its colors
darken and divide
as though stained; the green
patterning I thought lace
is its own, and the oily shine
comes back, and the sudden smell
of dizziness and sweat.

I could take it home
and plant it in a box;
I could talk about
what it did to me
and what I did to it,
or how in its element
it lives like you or me.
But it stops me, here
on my open hand,
by being a stone, and I send
it flying over the heads
of the fishing children,
arching alone above

the dialogue of reeds,
falling and falling toward water,
somewhere in water to strike
a conversation of stone.

¡HOLA MIGUELIN!

I

The night is rising in the young grass—
before noon and the land wind
sways through the fields. Along the trunk
of each blade, a juice rising
toward the pale crown.

I shut my eyes and imagine
a black dried bough of olive.
I bend it. When it gives
with a dry cough
a fine dust rises into our nostrils.

II

She stumbles into the noon—this morning
she was a shy wife—and the young
coarse wine that numbs
her arms and cools the sweat on
her forehead is summer itself.

If she goes forward she does so
from side to side
on her long delicate legs, bearing
herself between them, a faint
musk, a crown of curls, a gift
for the night that is always rising.

TWILIGHT

October. From Simpson's hill
the great moon of stone
frowns in the rain. In the
fields below dark bruises
of spike stiffen into seed.
The cows are shuffling
behind me, back down
to the long chromium sheds
and the painless taking.

I watch an hour pass.
The darkness rises from
the floor of the valley
thickening the air between
branches, between stone
and tree, between my eyes
and what was here.

Now I'm in the dark.
I remember pages torn
from an automotive catalogue,
an ad once fallen from
heaven and hanging in
the city air—"It's never too late . . ."
If I follow my hands
will I feel the winter shake
the almonds into blossom?

TO A FISH HEAD FOUND ON THE BEACH NEAR MÁLAGA

I

Flat, eventless afternoon
searching among the stones for nothing
I come upon the fish head.
                                                "¡Hola!"
Right off, head to head, with this
wide-eyed, unlistening remnant
of dead metal trailing its single
stiff feather of flesh.
                                    We talk of loneliness,
of the fear of stones falling like rain,
hatred of water tumbling out of dreams
and filling our small rooms. Shafts of sand
sifting under doors, filming
first the glasses, then the eyes,
weighing down the lips, the cry.

II

                                                Here, halfway
from home, I discover my head, its hideous
King Tongue going. My good hands explore it,
the hair thinning, the eyes scratched
and hot, that let the lids thump down,
and the poor muscles, unsleeping,
as burned as drawn ropes.
Only the chin happy, hidden in fur.

III

But how good to find companionship
of any kind. Fish head and man head,
communing in their tongue, an iron yawn
out over the waves, the one poem born
of the eternal and always going back.
I throw the fish head to the sea.
Let it be fish once more.
                                        I sniff my fingers
and catch the burned essential oil
seeping out of death. Out of beginning,
I hear, under the sea roar, the bone words
of teeth tearing earth and sea,
anointing the tongues with stone and sand,
water eating fish, fish water,
head eating head to let us be.

SALAMI

Stomach of goat, crushed
sheep balls, soft full
pearls of pig eyes,
snout gristle, fresh earth,
worn iron of trotter, slate
of Zaragoza, dried cat heart,
cock claws. She grinds
them with one hand and
with the other fists
mountain thyme, basil,
paprika, and knobs of garlic.
And if a tooth of stink thistle
pulls blood from the round
blue marbled hand
all the better for
this ruby of Pamplona,
this bright jewel of Vich,
this stained crown
of Solsona, this
salami.
                    The daughter
of mismatched eyes,
36 year old infant smelling
of milk. Mama, she cries, mama,
but mama is gone,
and the old stone cutter
must wipe the drool
from her jumper. His puffed fingers
unbutton and point her
to toilet. Ten, twelve hours
a day, as long as the winter sun
holds up he rebuilds
the unvisited church
of San Martin. Cheep cheep
of the hammer high above
the town, sparrow cries
lost in the wind or lost

in the mind. At dusk he leans
to the coal dull wooden Virgin
and asks for blessings on
the slow one and peace
on his grizzled head, asks
finally and each night
for the forbidden, for
the knowledge of every
mysterious stone, and
the words go out on
the overwhelming incense
of salami.

A single crow
passed high over the house,
I wakened out of nightmare.
The winds had changed,
the Tremontana was tearing
out of the Holy Mountains
to meet the sea winds
in my yard, burning and
scaring the young pines.
The single poplar wailed
in terror. With salt,
with guilt, with the need
to die, the vestments
of my life flared, I
was on fire, a stranger
staggering through my house
butting walls and falling
over furniture, looking
for a way out. In the last room
where moonlight slanted
through a broken shutter
I found my smallest son
asleep or dead, floating
on a bed of colorless light.
When I leaned closer

I could smell the small breaths
going and coming, and each
bore its prayer for me,
the true and earthy prayer
of salami.

II

CRY FOR NOTHING

1.

Make the stream
on the hurt faces
of stones, up the hillside
into the black house
of firs. Say
your name to stump,
to silence, to the sudden wings
of the air, say
your name to yourself.
It doesn't matter cause
it all comes back
a red leaf prick
in your crotch, burr balls
tapping at your ankles
with their Me! Me!
the fresh weed tongue lashing
at your cheek
to make you cry
for nothing.

2.

Motor roar of bad clutch, passing
goats, drunk trucks,
cement haulers, night men
coming home on foot, dawn men
going out
and steaming in anger
at the cold. Mark sleeps
next to me, his blond
woman hair tangling
the gear shift, behind
the little ones
breathing in their
bad socks, farting
and gnashing at
the first sex dreams,
and the mama, my alone
woman rolling in the limbo
of sleep. I'm awake
and staring
for the first breaks of light
between the prisoned towers
of hell slums north
of Barcelona and the dark tear pools
left in the streets.

3.
He let her drive
and she crashed her poppa's
front porch. Man
asked for her license
and she 14. The evening
gathering above the wooden
roofs, a heavy darkness
spreading from car lights.
Time to go. Small kids
near the kitchen asking,
and the oven flashing
its magic. Time to go
if you got a place
to go. Man let Luther,
and he called home, her
mother say she gone
early and the baby
be coming by now and
where is he.
                    He with me
pushing the old black Lincoln
back down the drive
watching the radiator bare
its muddy wounds. Luther
rolling his sleeves up
high and cupping his long
hillbilly fingers around
a flaring match, Luther
cocking his tattoo
against the black rain and
the rain of black luck, Luther
pushing on toward
the jewelled service station
of free cokes
and credit there ahead
in a heaven of blue

falling and nothing
going to make him cry
for nothing.

COMING HOME, *Detroit*, 1968

A winter Tuesday, the city pouring fire,
Ford Rouge sulfurs the sun, Cadillac, Lincoln,
Chevy gray. The fat stacks
of breweries hold their tongues. Rags,
papers, hands, the stems of birches
dirtied with words.
                                        Near the freeway
you stop and wonder what came off,
recall the snowstorm where you lost it all,
the wolverine, the northern bear, the wolf
caught out, ice and steel raining
from the foundries in a shower
of human breath. On sleds in the false sun
the new material rests. One brown child
stares and stares into your frozen eyes
until the lights change and you go
forward to work. The charred faces, the eyes
boarded up, the rubble of innards, the cry
of wet smoke hanging in your throat,
the twisted river stopped at the color of iron.
We burn this city every day.

DETROIT GREASE SHOP POEM

Four bright steel crosses,
universal joints, plucked
out of the burlap sack—
"the heart of the drive train"—
the book says. Stars
on Lemon's wooden palm,
stars that must be capped,
rolled, and annointed,
that have their orders
and their commands as he
has his.

Under the blue
hesitant light another day
at Automotive
in the city of dreams.
We're all there to count
and be counted, Lemon,
Rosie, Eugene, Luis,
and me, too young to know
this is for keeps, pinning
on my apron, rolling up
my sleeves.

The roof leaks
from yesterday's rain,
the waters gather above us
waiting for one mistake.
When a drop falls on Lemon's
corded arm, he looks at it
as though it were something
rare or mysterious
like a drop of water or
a single lucid meteor
fallen slowly from
nowhere and burning on
his skin like a tear.

THE ANGELS OF DETROIT

I

I could hear them in fever
hovering in the closet or
falling from the mirror. I
could see them in the first dreams
of my dead.
                        Perfume of scorched
clothes . . . she spits back
at the spitting iron, she slaps
it with a round pink palm
and the angels sigh
from the shadowy valleys
of my shirts.

II

I wore angels.
They saved me in the streets
where the towers hung above
suspended on breath, they
saved me from the pale woman
who smoothed the breasts
of chickens or the red-armed
one who sold bread in
the shop of knives.

While I leaned
on the cold stones of summer
and tried to cry and tried
to change they sent me
a robed mother or a
promise in the dark hall.
In the black river at midnight
they said, Go back!

They sent snow
to cover the steps, to crown
the teeth of garbage and bless
the deaths of old cars, snow
falling on our upturned faces
in the great church, the presses
choiring in the roof of night.

III

From Toledo by bus,
from Flat Rock on syphoned gas,
from the iron country on
a dare. For one night.
Stash says, Nigger
boy's crying in
the shit house.

All of us far from
momma and gettin farther.

IV

At the end of mud road
in the false dawn of the slag heap
the hut of the angel Bernard.
His brothers are factories and
bowling teams, his mother is the
power to blight, his father
moves in all men like a threat,
a closing of hands, an unkept
promise to return.
                                        We talk
for years; everything we
say comes to nothing. We drink
bad beer and never lie. From
his bed he pulls fists
of poems and scatters them
like snow. "Children are guilty,"
he whispers, and the soft mouth
puffs like a wound.

He wants it all tonight.
The long hard arms of a black woman,
he wants tenderness, he wants
the power to die in the
chalice of God's tears.

True dawn through the soaped window.
The plastic storm-wrap swallows wind.
'37 Chevie hoodless, black burst
lung of inner tube, pot metal
trees buckling under sheets.
He cries to sleep.

V

In a toilet on Joy Rd
long Eddie on alto.
The yellows of his eyes
brown on pot, the brown centers
burned like washed gold.

Never knew the tune. 16
years old, drummer
had to prod him to music.
So much sorrow in hatred,
so much tenderness
he could taste coming up
from the rich earth.

Little clown. Caught all alone,
arm in a mail-box.
Never did nothing right
except tell the cops to suck
and wave them off like flies.

VI

After midnight of the final
shift, with all our prayers
unanswered, we gave up.
Unvisored pale knot of
West Virginia, mountain rock and
black valley earth, ungloved
yellow potato, dried tubers,
yoked bean, frozen cedars
of weariness, we gave up.

The cranes slip
overhead. The ore pours
from the earth to us, poor earth
somewhere unseamed. If you
listen quiet to Lonnie
next to you or hopping Sugar
you can hear it
piping in pity.

Don't matter what rare breath
puddles in fire on
the foundry floor. The toilets
overflow, the rats dance, the maggots
have it, the worms of money
crack like whips, and
among the angels
we lie down.

VII

Red haired black skinned
Cuban woman. Wait all night
in the parking lot. Doze and talk—
to no one—of home. The panels
of the black chapel flame,
the glass melts or races
with stars. Nothing lasts
forever. Sun up shatters
the yellowed windows of the old Dodge.
She meets us, coatless, in magenta,
an early flower late blooming
in the fenced white wastes,
bare arms open.

SATURDAY SWEEPING

Saturday sweeping
with an old broom
counting the strokes
back and forth.
The dust sprays
up silver in the
February sun
and comes down gray.
Soft straw muzzle
poking in and
bringing out
scraps of news,
little fingers
and signatures.
Everybody's
had this room
one time or another
and never thought
to sweep. Outside
the snows stiffen,
the roofs loosen
their last teeth
into the streets.
Outside it's
1952,
Detroit, unburned,
stumbles away
from my window
over the drained roofs
toward the river
to scald its useless
hands. Half
the men in this town
are crying in
the snow, their eyes
blackened like
Chinese soldiers.

The gates are closing
at Dodge Main
and Wyandotte
Chemical; they
must go home
to watch the kids
scrub their brown
faces or grease
cartridges for
the show down.
If anyone knocks
on your door
he'll be
oil flecked or
sea born, he'll
be bringing word
from the people
of the ice drifts
or the great talking dogs
that saved the Jews.
Meanwhile our masters
will come on
television
to ask for our help.
Here, the radiator's
working, stove says
Don't touch,
and the radio's crying,
I don't get enough.
I'm my keeper,
the only thing
I've got,
sweeping out
my one-room life
while the sun's
still up.

ANGEL BUTCHER

At sun up I am up
hosing down the outdoor abattoir
getting ready. The water
steams and hisses on the white stones
and the air pales to a
thin blue.
Today it is
Christophe. I don't see him
come up the long climb or
know he's here until I hear
my breathing double
and he's beside me smiling
like a young girl.
He asks
me the names of all
the tools and all
their functions, he lifts
and weighs and
balances, and runs a long
forefinger down the tongue
of each blade.
He asks
me how I came to this place and
this work, and I tell him how
I began with animals, and
he tells me how
he began with animals. We
talk about growing up and losing
the strange things we never
understood and settling.
I help
him with his robes; he
has a kind of modesty and sits
on the stone table with
the ends of the gown crossed
in his lap.

He wants to die
like a rabbit, and he wants me
to help him. I hold
his wrist; it's small, like
the throat of a young hen, but
cool and dry. He holds
mine and I can feel the
blood thudding in the ring
his fingers make.
He helps me, he
guides my hand at first. I can
feel my shoulders settle and
the bones take the weight, I can
feel my lungs flower as the
swing begins. He smiles again
with only one side of his mouth
and looks down to the
dark valley where the cities
burn. When I hit
him he comes apart like a
perfect puzzle or an
old flower.
And my legs
dance and twitch for hours.

THEY FEED THEY LION

Out of burlap sacks, out of bearing butter,
Out of black bean and wet slate bread,
Out of the acids of rage, the candor of tar,
Out of creosote, gasoline, drive shafts, wooden dollies,
They Lion grow.
                    Out of the gray hills
Of industrial barns, out of rain, out of bus ride,
West Virginia to Kiss My Ass, out of buried aunties,
Mothers hardening like pounded stumps, out of stumps,
Out of the bones' need to sharpen and the muscles' to stretch,
They Lion grow.
                    Earth is eating trees, fence posts,
Gutted cars, earth is calling in her little ones,
"Come home, Come home!" From pig balls,
From the ferocity of pig driven to holiness,
From the furred ear and the full jowl come
The repose of the hung belly, from the purpose
They Lion grow.
                    From the sweet glues of the trotters
Come the sweet kinks of the fist, from the full flower
Of the hams the thorax of caves,
From "Bow Down" come "Rise Up,"
Come they Lion from the reeds of shovels,
The grained arm that pulls the hands,
They Lion grow.
                    From my five arms and all my hands,
From all my white sins forgiven, they feed,
From my car passing under the stars,
They Lion, from my children inherit,
From the oak turned to a wall, they Lion,
From they sack and they belly opened
And all that was hidden burning on the oil-stained earth
They feed they Lion and he comes.

III

ALONE

Sunset, and the olive grove flames
on the far hill. We descend
into the lunging shadows
of goat grass, and the air

deepens like smoke.
You were behind me, but when I turned
there was the wrangling of crows
and the long grass rising in the wind

and the swelling tips of grain
turning to water under a black sky.
All around me the thousand
small denials of the day

rose like insects to the flaming
of an old truth, someone alone
following a broken trail of stones
toward the deep and starless river.

AUTUMN

Out of gas south
of Ecorse. In the dark
I can smell the dogs
circling behind the
wrecked cars.
                                On a sidestreet,
unlighted, we find a
new Chevy. I suck
the tube until
my mouth fills
and cools with new
American wine.

———

Old man says,
Elephant moves slow, tortoise
don't hardly move at all and they
has no trouble to be
a hundrid.
                              The small
ladders of hair dangle
from his nostrils, hands
peppered like old eggs.

———

I left you in Washington,
honey, and went to Philly. All the
way beside the tracks, empires
of metal shops, brickflats, storage tanks,
robbing the air.
                                        Later, behind
barbed wire, I found small arms
swaddled in cosmoline, tanks, landing
craft, half tracks smiling
through lidded eyes,
grenades blooming in
their beds.
                              April,
1954, we've got each other
in a borrowed room.

———

Who comes before dawn through
the drifts of dried leaves
to my door? The clawed gopher,
the egret lost on his way, the inland
toad, the great
Pacific tortoise?
                                        I rise
from a warm bed and go and
find nothing, not a neighbor
armed and ready, not a cop
not even my own son
deserting.
                              I stand
in a circle of light, my heart
pounding and pounding at the door
of its own wilderness.

———

Snow steaming on the still
warm body of the jackrabbit
shot and left, snow
on the black streets
melting, snow falling endlessly
on the great runways that
never fill.
                    The twentieth autumn
of our war, the dead heart
and the living clogged
in snow.
                A small clearing
in the pines, the wind
talking through the high trees,
we have water, we
have air, we have bread, we have
a rough shack whitening,
we have snow on your eyelids,
on your hair.

ANGEL 14

He passes into the streets in a business suit,
he crosses at the corner where the children wait
on their way to the fenced yards and the dark barns.

The first snow falls dusting the raw faces
of the oak stumps, the first snow thickens like paste
between the slender fingers of the raccoon.

He lies face down on a rumpled bed and feels
creation ticking in his heart, ticking in his bowels,
he feels the blood and its rushing into black stones.

It's afternoon and once more the light is failing.
I won't serve, he says. His eyes are cups
that hold fists, hair pins, bombers,

the lost tooth a girl wrapped in cloth,
the old problems without solutions, the yellowing
pages read and reread, the circle drawn in dirt.

The muscles knot between my ribs, I carry an axe
and cut nothing, looking for dust I pour out milk.
Silver filings collect under fingernails,

nailed to the iron pond the egret eats its wings,
a child turns suddenly and crashes through glass
and passes into the streets in a business suit.

HOW MUCH CAN IT HURT?

The woman at the checkstand
Who wishes you cancer

The fat man who hates his mother
The doctor who forgets

The soup bubbling on the back of the stove
The stone staring into the sun

The girl who kisses her own arms
The girl who fries her hair

The egg turning brown under the spoon
The lemon laughing all night long

My brother in his uniform over Dresden
The single thrill of fire going for the bed

The kindergarten blowing its windows out
Chalk burning the little fingers

The newspaper waiting all weekend
Dozing in rain with the deaths smeared on its lips

The oiling and loading and the springing
The bullets sucking quietly in their cradles

How much can it hurt in the wood
In the long nerve of lead, in the fattened head

How much can it hurt
In each ration of meat hooked and hanging

In the unfinished letter, the dried opened socket
The veil of skin flapping, the star falling

My face punctured with glass
The teeth eating themselves in dreams

Our blood refusing to breathe, refusing to sleep
Asking the wounded moon

Asking the pillow, asking, asking
How much can it hurt?

THE CHILDREN'S CRUSADE

Crossbow wanted a child,
a little schoolboy with a red hole
in his brow

like the President. He excited
everyone. They made a brilliant
pair of angel's wings from Kaiser foil

and posterboard, they made a little
tufted box. They would cross his arms
on a single burning peony.

They'd get a glossy Testament,
a blanket tucked in
deep around the sides.

He wanted the little boy who skipped
all the way to school. Eve shook
her red head, and the silver

ignition keys hooked in her
pierced ears chirped. "No, No,"
he was going to be

her lover friend. She wanted
someone like Daddy. Archangel said,
"Daddy."

They took stations.
The night hollered through
the branches and the long grass

like a burned TV.
They bit their hands and waited.
Daddy's car closed.

Everything went quiet and they
had to still their heads like they'd learned
when the bedroom door opened.

After they stabbed him down,
Eve came out from
the shadows. She pulled his beard

but only a little came loose.
She stood so tall in mother's shoes,
and with blue and green chalk

on her lids and cheeks,
he never
knew her. He licked his lips

like when he said important
things, and spread his arms
and made his eyes make tears,

he wanted to talk, he wanted
to help them all, but she just pushed
the knife between his teeth.

When he stopped, they tried
to finish. The box was way too small
and he was too heavy.

So they giggled. When they smelled
what he'd done, they giggled
more. A Daddy going ka ka!

They rolled him over and tore
rags of skin from the eucalyptus
and hid him forever.

Now they ran. The shadows
were all gone, and the air
growing as soft as stone

underwater. Underwater or in moonlight,
the hills rose above the earth,
and they ran shedding their caps and bells,

the little silent bells
they wore at wrist and ankle,
they threw away their names and their no-names.

They cast their knives on the absent waters
and their long bamboo spears.
"Goodbye, rusty can opener, Goodbye!"

The houses were snapping.
It was over and they ran. Never
to wait! Now they were free.

LATER STILL

Two sons are gone.
The end of winter, and the almond blooms
near the back fence. The plum, slower,
unfolds under a streaked sky. The words become,
like prayer, a kind of nonsense
which becomes the thought of our lives.

In middle age we came
to the nine years war, the stars raged
in our horoscopes and the land
turned inwards biting for its heart.

Now in February the pussy willow
furs in the chill wind. In March
the sudden peach, cherry, lilac, in summer
the drumming gourd, corn, grape, and later still
the ghostly milkweed and the last laugh.

IV

THISTLES

for George Oppen

A MOUNTAIN THISTLE IN MARCH,
the stem a bitter green,
the blossom faded
like the stained robes
of martyrs.
                    Roots
spun through entrails
of the wakened earth
darkening into rocks
and the long nests.

The sun up long
past five, hanging
in a crown of gold.
—Take the mountain thistle—
it said.
                A film of snow
whirling from the thickets,
the new throats
of my fingers
streaked and itching.

IT'S AUGUST.
Dust sifts from the dark wings
of the magpie, the trails
flounder in sand.
A high wind in the tips
of the pines, without
a sigh the leaf on
my palm dies
into itself.
Somewhere
                    on this mountain
a truck gears down
and the rocks flake
into smaller and smaller lives.

I CLIMBED NINE FENCES THIS MORNING

haven't seen a cow or goat or horse or man . . .

In the center of a long meadow
try to sit still
the patient rocks staring
the sun stopped in
the pines assembled at the far edge
listening

Each time I lean my weight
on the top strand
something in me tears loose

How do I get out?

IF HE RAN
his long hair would fly
in the wind, if he sat still
his mind would run
with the names of rocks and trees
turned against him.

23 yr old draft dodger
he tracks the rim
of this sullen mountain lake.
He sent his girl away
he watched his Whitman, Rilke, Snyder
go up with the boathouse
a bright showering cage
against the night sky.

He feels the corners
of his mouth pull down,
his eyes vague.
Some old poet
would say, Bereft.
He thinks, Up Tight,
Fucked Over, trying to walk
inside my life.

IN THE CITY OF MY BIRTH

someone sees my eyes
and turns from the mirror
someone hears my voice
and shouts and shouts
to keep it out

At noon through the vacant squares
the sirens breathe
shuddering in each life
I lost

In the room I forgot
which I said I'd never forget
the mended bathrobe slips
to the floor,
the closet sags
with the sudden weights
of regret

The middle-aged press operator
curls on my bed
in his leather jacket
In the shadows
of the struck elm
the sparrows hush

Above on the 4th floor
the Appalachian widow
sings into the sink
until her sons come
one by one
to take the trees apart

DOWN THE MOUNTAIN
in Fresno, L.A., Oakland
a man with three names and no features
closes my file.
                                    The winds
are weighed, the distance clocked.
Everything is entered in the book.

HANGING ON IN THE MOON SOIL
north of Alicante
where even the rocks
can no longer sleep,
                                the cactus
dreams on the promise
of rain.
              Little pagan
villages of green spines
tenements of earthly joy.

And here and here
a thistle
like a fox leaps
toward the burning
filaments of shade.

THEY GO ON HITTING
flies and grounders.
The darkness rises
from the long grass
and pulls them in.

The last raw plume
of day breaks up
and flares out, when I
look back there's no one,
only a dark sea—

Somewhere out there
forests of antennas,
empty houses, trees, posts,
and cars, all
the closed presences
of this world

And the voices of kids
floating out and back.

My wife and I
stand wordless
on the chilled lawn
waiting for our sons
to come as they please,
to step suddenly out
of nothing, still warm,
grass smeared, robed
in their own songs.

THE BIG GUY RAN AND HID HIMSELF
in the can, and Mez and I
stayed and fought. Their drunkenness
uglier even than ours, their bodies
marvellous and no imagination to pull
their punches.
                                Upright to the hospital,
the shabby dignity of losers
who fought for nothing and
deserved everything we got.
                                                    7 years
later the big guy, rabbit-eyed
at quiet New York drink party,
shook my hand.
                                Friend, I didn't say,
we get our chance, it comes
round and it
comes round. Those twitch-nosed
academic pants-pisser poets
of the 50's will take up
against the State,
and you'll be with us,
Mother.

RISES IN THE DARK
fixes coffee
hands moving like starlings
above the glowing electric rings.

Outside a mockingbird snaps
from the sycamore
the branch sways
and calms

60 yr old wanderer
he sits in the dark
in my chair, plotting
the next move, the poem

—Tool & Die past,
L.A. backyard cabinetshop
& no loyalty oath
8 yrs Mexico woodlathe—

Always a new dark
the cup nests in the stained hands
the mockingbird returns
the tree returns.

THE DAWN FOX

high on the meth of
drugged chickens
attacks dog, gophers, hoses,
tricycle tires.
                    If they knew
he was here they'd hunt
him on horseback among
the abandoned cars
in The Hollywood Hills'
Wilderness, they'd
make a game of it
drinking his death in
Pepsi,
            his death who rode
the shield of Lucca up the impossible
Etruscan slopes, who turned
to fight the pig mounted Archers
of the Moon.
                    Tearing his
yellowed eyes through the screen door
to get the house cat.

THE THISTLE
torn off and brought down
admired
and tossed on a shelf

All night the jets hammering
above the house
all night the thistle
opening and opening

and now the first sun
flooding

everyone breathing
his own life

the house living

the refrigerator's
even pulsing
the water heater
yawning and
popping

the east windows
rubbed
open on the quicksilver
of the eucalyptus

Not snow but
seeds fallen
through the roof
of my life
on the stained table
the glass
the silent phone
the unanswerable letter

V

DARK RINGS

Young Teddy holds his face
away from the water, tips
his fingers with soap
and washes. The fine hairs
along the jaw darken,
the neck darkens day after day,
and he will not take
off his shirt even to sleep.

———

Who hears my prayers? 8 hrs
plating toilet fixtures, and now
midnight snows on Bagley Ave.
Let the bus come, let the small deposits
of nickel, the flakes of copper
blacken around the heart, let
it be tomorrow. I talk only
to stars, they're coming down too.

———

Between the lost breath
of the fir trees and the air,
a blue smear. Tinged with
yellow, it is a fire
cleaning the way
of sighs in which they name
themselves.
                        3000 ft
below, the day ends in ashes,
in particles of blood streaming
from the eyes of trucks.

———

It will rain today. I waken
hearing the sea, the howl
of old glass against
the wind. The fisherman
upstairs will not get up.
His wife begs, his
daughter cries. The sea wind
breaks again around
my bed with its cargo
of salt, fish tap at
the glass, and laughing
we are underway toward
the black dawning.

Heart of the cottonwood
I chopped in October. The red ants
streaming away from the face
of the axe. A dark soft year,
I trace it with my finger, a year
when the grasses turned
downward and poured into
the roots, a year still
in the white yielding heart.

All night in
the bus station in Chicago
afraid to go out, saw
a cabdriver throw
a woman into the street, saw
her hat like a circle
of blood burning
the snow, the snow sobbing
out of the mouths
of oil drums. When I stopped at last
in the alley and listened
my heart was silent
and a river of broken glass
moved under my feet.

The Bear dozes off
in a dust of stars. I walk
in winter orchards
and the earth creaks
underfoot. No moon and no light
overflowing the black sockets
of the fig. My right fist
pops like a cinder
in the cold. The sun hangs
under the rim of night
waiting for the world.

THE WAY DOWN

On the way down
blue lupin at the roadside,
red bud scattered
down the mountain, tiny
white jump-ups hiding
underfoot, the first push
of wild oats like froth
at the field's edge. The wind blows
through everything, the crowned
peaks above us, the soft floor
of the valley below,
the humps of rock
walking down the world.

On the way down
from the trackless snow fields
where a blackbird
eyed me from
a solitary pine, knowing
I would go back the way
I came, shaking my head,
and the blue glitter of ice
was like the darkness
of winter nights, deepening
before it could change,
and the only voice
my own saying
Goodbye.

Can you hear me?
the air says. I hold
my breath and listen
and a finger of dirt thaws,
a river drains
from a snow drop
and rages down
my cheeks, our father
the wind hums
a prayer through my mouth
and answers in the oat,
and now the tight rows of seed
bow to the earth
and hold on and hold on.

WAKING IN ALICANTE

Driven all day over bad roads
  from Barcelona, down
    the coast. The heat

murderous, the air clogged with dust,
  to arrive at evening
    in Alicante, city

of dim workers' quarters, bad trucks,
  furious little bars
    and the same heat.

I awaken at 4, tasting fried calamares
  and the salty beer the sea
    has given us,

tasting the bitterness of all the lives
  around me in the darkness
    fumbling toward dawn.

My smallest son, on the same narrow
  bed, his knees pumping
    sporadically

as though he ran into the blackness
  of sleep away from all
    that sleep is not—

the dark creased women that hover
  above each soiled turnip,
    each stained onion,

that bleed the bread sour with their thumbs,
  the old beaten soldiers in ruined
    suits, dying

in the corners of bus stations, talking
  in bars to no one, making
    the night roads

to nowhere, and the long gray-legged boys
  hiding their tears
    behind cupped hands.

How much anger and shame falls slowly
  like rain into his life
    to nurture

the strange root that is the heart
  of a boy growing
    to manhood.

It grows in the shape I give it
  each day, a man,
    a poet

in middle age still wandering in search
  of that boy's dream
    of a single self

formed of all the warring selves split
  off at my birth
    and set spinning.

The slate hills rising from the sea,
  the workers' fortress I saw
    bathed in dust,

the rifle loops crumbling like dead mouths,
  the little promontory
    where the deaths

were done thirty years ago, the death
still hanging in the burning
air, are mine.

Now I have come home to Spain, home
to my Spanish self
for this one night.

The bats still circle the streetlight
outside my window
until the first

gray sifting of dawn startles their eyes
and the motorcycles start
up, rocketing

down the high narrow streets.
Teddy stirs next
to me, a life

awakening once again to all the lives
raging in the streets,
and to his own.

Who will he be today, this child
of mine, this fair
and final child?

The eyes dart under soft lids
and open and the world
once more

is with him, and he smiles at me,
the father welcoming
him home.

TO P.L., 1916–1937

a soldier of the Republic

Gray earth peeping through snow,
you lay for three days
with one side of your face
frozen to the ground. They tied your cheek
with the red and black scarf
of the Anarchists, and bundled you
in canvas, and threw you away.
Before that an old country woman
of the Aragon, spitting on her thumb,
rubbing it against her forefinger,
stole your black Wellingtons,
the gray hunting socks, and the long
slender knife you wore
in a little leather scabbard
riding your right hip. She honed it,
ran her finger down the blade, and laughed,
though she had no meat to cut,
blessing your tight fists
that had fallen side by side
like frozen faces on your hard belly
that was becoming earth. (Years later
she saw the two faces
at table, and turned from the bread
and the steaming oily soup, turned
to the darkness of the open door,
and opened her eyes to darkness
that they might be filled with anything
but those two faces squeezed
in the blue of snow and snow and snow.)
She blessed your feet, still pink,
with hard yellow shields of skin
at heel and toe, and she laughed
scampering across the road, into
the goat field, and up the long hill,
the boots bundled in her skirts,
and the gray hunting socks, and the knife.

To P.L., 1916–1937

For seven weeks she wore the boots
stuffed with rags at toe and heel.
She thought she understood
why you lay down to rest
even in snow, and gave them to a nephew,
and the gray socks too.
The knife is still used, the black handle
almost white, the blade
worn thin since there is meat to cut.
Without laughter she is gone
ten years now,
and on the road to Huesca in spring
there is no one to look for you
among the wild jonquils, the curling
grasses at the road side,
and the blood red poppies, no one
to look on the farthest tip
of wind breathing down from the mountains
and shaking the stunted pines you hid among.

BREATH

Who hears the humming
of rocks at great height,
the long steady drone
of granite holding together,
the strumming of obsidian
to itself? I go among
the stones stooping
and pecking like a
sparrow, imagining
the glacier's final push
resounding still. In
a freezing mountain
stream, my hand opens
scratched and raw and
flutters strangely,
more like an animal
or wild blossom in wind
than any part of me. Great
fields of stone
stretching away under
a slate sky, their single
flower the flower
of my right hand.
                                        Last night
the fire died into itself
black stick by stick
and the dark came out
of my eyes flooding
everything. I
slept alone and dreamed
of you in an old house
back home among
your country people,
among the dead, not
any living one besides
yourself. I woke

scared by the gasping
of a wild one, scared
by my own breath, and
slowly calmed
remembering your weight
beside me all these
years, and here and
there an eye of stone
gleamed with the warm light
of an absent star.
                    Today
in this high clear room
of the world, I squat
to the life of rocks
jewelled in the stream
or whispering
like shards. What fears
are still held locked
in the veins till the last
fire, and who will calm
us then under a gold sky
that will be all of earth.
Two miles below on the burning
summer plains, you go
about your life one
more day. I give you
almond blossoms
for your hair, your hair
that will be white, I give
the world my worn-out breath
on an old tune, I give
it all I have
and take it back again.

THE NAMES OF THE LOST

For Buenaventura Durruti (1896–1936)
and the world he said is growing here
in my heart this moment

ON THE BIRTH OF GOOD & EVIL DURING THE LONG WINTER OF '28

When the streetcar stalled on Joy Road,
the conductor finished his coffee, puffed
into his overcoat, and went to phone in.
The Hungarian punch-press operator wakened
alone, 7000 miles from home, pulled down
his orange cap and set out. If he saw
the winter birds scuffling in the cinders,
if he felt this was the dawn of a new day,
he didn't let on. Where the sidewalks
were unshovelled, he stamped on, raising
his galoshes a little higher with each step.
I came as close as I dared and could hear
only the little gasps as the cold entered
the stained refectory of the breath.
I could see by the way the blue tears squeezed
from the dark of the eyes, by the way
his moustache first dampened and then froze,
that as he turned down Dexter Boulevard,
he considered the hosts of the dead,
and nearest among them, his mother-in-law,
who darkened his table for twenty-seven years
and bruised his wakings. He considered how
before she went off in the winter of '27
she had knitted this cap, knitted so slowly
that Christmas came and went, and now he could
forgive her at last for the twin wool lappets
that closed perfectly on a tiny metal snap
beneath the chin and for making all of it orange.

THE SECRET OF THEIR VOICES

When they wakened
in the gray
of just after dawn
and knew the birds
were gone and saw
the diesel fumes
gathering above the trees
and felt the cold anger
of machines that have to eat,
did they come hand
in hand through
the bare wood halls
to sway above my bed
and call me back
to the small damp body
curled in dream?

He pulled the long socks
up and eased his feet
into the narrow shoes,
tied the laces, and stood
staring down the hard creases.
Roses are blooming
in Picardeee, she sang,
and looked sideways
at her self in the mirror
drawing her cheeks in.
But there's only one
rose for me, and stood
smoothing the wrinkles
from waist to knee.

If they left,
whose hand cupped
my forehead when I lay
in fever? Who moaned,
help me, help me?

Who lay full length
beside me, belted and all,
and let his tears
pour over my hands?
Who huddled beside me
whispering like a sleepwalker
in the wet grove
north of Anniston?
Tell me! Tell me! Tell me!
I might have helped.

ELEGY FOR TEDDY HOLMES, DEAD IN A FAR LAND

I

Here the air takes the host
of the air, rain tipped with ether
and a wafer of smoke.
It is August and you are gone
two years into the earth.
Near the cold source the streams
thicken with froth, the hawk—
who is your laughter—
wakens, his wings glued
to the high cedar branch.

If she were alive, my Aunt Tsipie
would say a prayer against your going
(you were so much alike
with your dark heads of patience,
your large hands,
and the smiles pinched at the end).
She would hold your book
unopened, and nod that she knew
nothing of such things,
and go on dressing the child,
who in middle age can't count her fingers.
All the playmates went off
and sent back tall ugly strangers
and some like you sent no one.

II

Your wife writes us about the end,
she doesn't say how the larks
fled down the lanes
of the broken grove,
she doesn't say how the table
sighed under her palms
when she begged to hold you
and was denied,
she doesn't say how she walked

out alone after dinner
past the open windows
where the girls sewed and mended,
past the station of closed shutters
where the cop dozed in a green cape,
how she heard the chant of the seashell,
the muttering of chalk,
how where water was black
and each drop burned
she pledged in this odd tongue
and was frightened.

III
Our fathers gone forever and apart
into the lies of the city,
our mothers stunned in the schoolrooms
before the sudden blood of men and boys,
the eyes of animals, the skin
of girls burning like raw opal,
how clearly you saw it all.

And at the end you saw the earth tip
and barns and trees and old rusted trucks
slide away,
the fields peel away,
and then the dry clay
underneath us all, the drawn brow
of an old woman, tired
of being called each night
to bring wine to the grown ones,
water to the young.

NO ONE REMEMBERS

A soft wind
off the stones of the dead.
I pass by, stop the car,
and walk among none
of my own, to say
something useless
for them, something
that will calm me under
the same old beaten sky,
something to let me
go on with this day
that began so badly
alone in a motel 10 miles
from where I was born.

I say *Goodbye* finally
because nothing else is here,
because it is Goodbye,
Uncle Joe, big cigar, fist
on the ear, nodding *sure*
bitch and coming at me.
You can't touch me now,
and she's a thousand miles
from here, hell, she may be
dancing long past dawn
across the river
from Philly. It's morning
there too, even in Philly,
it's morning on Lake St. Clair
where we never went fishing,
along the Ohio River, the Detroit,
morning breaking on
the New York Central Express
crashing through the tunnel
and the last gasp of steam
before the entrance into hell
or Baltimore, but it's not

morning where you are, Joe,
unless you come with me.

I'm going to see her today.
She'll cry like always
when you raised your voice
or your fist, she'll
be robed near the window
of the ward when I come in.
No, she won't be dancing.
It's my hand she'll take
in hers and spread on her lap,
it's me she'll feel
slowly finger by finger
like so many threads back
to where the blood died
and our lives met
and went wrong, back
to all she said she'd be,
woman, promise, sigh,
dark hair in the mirror
of a car window all night
on the way back from Georgia.

You think because I
was a boy, I didn't hear,
you think because you had
a pocketful of loose change,
your feet on the desk,
your own phone, a yellow car
on credit, I didn't see
you open your hands
like a prayer and die
into them the way a child
dies into a razor, black hair,
into a tire iron, a chain.
You think I didn't smell

the sweat that rose
from your bed, didn't
know you on the stairs
in the dark, grunting
into a frightened girl.
Because you could push me
aside like a kitchen chair
and hit where you wanted,
you think I was a wren,
a mourning dove
surrendering the nest.

The earth is asleep, Joe,
it's rock, steel, ice,
the earth doesn't care
or forgive. No one remembers
your eyes before they tired,
the way you fought weeping.
No one remembers how much
it cost to drive all night
to Chicago, how much
to sleep all night in a car,
to have it all except
the money. No one remembers
your hand, opened, warm
and sweating on the back
of my neck when you first
picked me up and said
my name, *Philip,* and held
the winter sun up
for me to see outside
the French windows of
the old house on Pingree,
no one remembers.

YOU

The moon gone dark
in the smoke of the rolling mills,
the switch engines quiet
in the iron sheds.
On our last break we smoked
in silence, the night cool at last
in its last hour.
When your head dropped to your chest
I parted your fingers
and drew the cigarette out
and smoked it.

A thousand years away
our father lay down
in the hymning shade of the olives
and dreamed of that road
twisting back,
and he wakened in the world.

A box car rasped.
I blinked the poor light
of another day, all around me
the houses had started.
In bare kitchens
men bowed
to coffee and cold porridge.
You were gone, brother,
the face I never saw in darkness
gone, the cigarette gone,
and I haven't touched you since.

NEW SEASON

My son and I go walking in the garden.
It is April 12, Friday, 1974.
Teddy points to the slender trunk
of the plum and recalls the digging
last fall through three feet
of hard pan and opens his palms
in the brute light of noon, the heels
glazed with callus, the long fingers
thicker than mine and studded with
silver rings. My mother is 70 today.
He flicks two snails off a leaf
and smashes them underfoot
on the red brick path. Saturday,
my wife stood here, her cheek cut
by a scar of dirt, dirt on her bare
shoulders, on the brown belly,
damp and sour in the creases
of her elbows. She held up a parsnip
squat, misshapen, a tooth pulled
from the earth, and laughed
her great white laugh. Teddy talks
of the wars of the young, Larry V.
and Ricky's brother in the movies,
on Belmont, at McDonald's,
ready to fight for nothing, hard,
redded or on air, "low riders,
grease, what'd you say about my mama!"
Home late, one in the back seat,
his fingers broken, eyes welling
with pain, the eyes and jawbones
swollen and rough. 70 today, the woman
who took my hand and walked me
past the corridor of willows
to the dark pond where the one swan
drifted. I start to tell him
and stop, the story of my 15th spring.
That a sailor had thrown a black baby

off the Belle Isle Bridge was
the first lie we heard, and the city
was at war for real. We would waken
the next morning to find Sherman tanks
at the curb and soldiers camped
on the lawns. Damato said he was
"goin downtown bury a hatchet
in a nigger's head." Women
took coffee and milk to the soldiers
and it was one long block party
till the trucks and tanks loaded up
and stumbled off. No one saw
Damato for a week, and when I did
he was slow, head down, his right arm
blooming in a great white bandage.
He said nothing. On mornings I rise
early, I watch my son in the bathroom,
shirtless, thick-armed and hard,
working with brush and comb
at his full blond head that suddenly
curled like mine and won't
come straight. 7 years passed
before Della Daubien told me
how three white girls from the shop
sat on her on the Woodward Streetcar
so the gangs couldn't find her
and pull her off like they did
the black janitor and beat
an eye blind. She would never
forget, she said, and her old face
glows before me in shame
and terror. Tonight, after dinner,
after the long, halting call
to my mother, I'll come out here
to the yard rinsed in moonlight
that blurs it all. She will not
become the small openings

in my brain again through which the wind
rages, though she was the ocean
that ebbed in my blood, the storm clouds
that battered my lungs, though I hide
in the crotch of the orange tree
and weep where the future grows
like a scar, she will not come again
in the brilliant day. My cat Nellie,
15 now, follows me, safe
in the dark from mockingbird
and jay, her fur frost tipped
in the pure air, and together we hear
the wounding of the rose, the willow
on fire—to the dark pond
where the one swan drifted, the woman
is 70 now—the willow is burning,
the rhododendrons shrivel
like paper under water, all
the small secret mouths are feeding
on the green heart of the plum.

AUTUMN AGAIN

The flowers drying
in the garden are
the body. My wife
raises the fallen arm
and binds the forehead.
She goes on her knees
before a rose blackened
at the center, she rests
in the shadow of sunflower.
At 8:30 there is a carnival
of blue morning glories;
the mockingbird squawks
their sudden thoughts,
the hummingbird steals
their intuitions. If I love
the body that is yours
for a time, wild phlox,
marigold, weed, if I love
the cactus that holds on
and the thistle burning
alone, if we are
our bodies, naked
in the sun of 'Tater Hill,
tipped with sweat
and chilled in the winds,
will we come at last
to dirt and stone and love them?
I ask with this tongue
which makes words and is
itself a word, this breath
humming among the 22
graves of my mouth.
If the body's hair
moves in a slow dance, one
part fire, three parts
water, if the eye
is an island that beholds

do we therefore say,
"You are the apple
of my eye?" First cold
morning in September
on a rock overlooking
Lake Huron. I said,
"It ends here." A wild horse,
I might have run
where the fields pulled.
I might have prayed for wings
and flown. Remembering,
I laugh. I back my car
out over the grass, I
slow on 41 to avoid
the smear of possum,
I pass the schoolyard
with its fence of spikes
and broken glass. I work
today, head down at my desk,
not daring to look out for fear
there will be snow falling
and each flake must be counted.
Among all the letters, one
from my mother. She has lost
her name, can I tell her
how she was born and came
to be in Los Angeles.
Do I recall the lilacs
she passed each morning,
the mock orange I planted
to please her and how
it sprang up like corn,
how the children grew
and thickened like August days,
how each was one more
small charge against the sky.
If I held her head now

it would be clay,
it would be a clear ache
of blue. If I asked why,
my tongue would curl back
and be swallowed. Covered
with dust, rags over
their mouths, our sisters
go out in open trucks
to burn in the fields.
Everyone inches up or down,
step by step. The heart
of a peach glows on its tree,
at dusk a worm calls itself
by a name no one knows.
Everyone brings some piece
of himself to the table,
and the old wood groans.
Even I heal and become
new again. Under the scab
the skin is pink and shiny,
and though the hand kinks
until the fingers are a cup
of five pains that once held
water and flesh, I will sleep
and waken by the road
below the Renault garage.
Down the oiled path of cans
and innertubes in the field
by the river, the young
mechanic ties up his beans
at dawn, weeds his herb garden
fenced with string, marjoram,
costmary, dill, and worships
one more than another
because they are his.

WEDNESDAY

I could say the day began
behind the Sierras,
in the orange grove the ladder
that reaches partway
to the stars grew
a shadow, and the fruit
wet with mist put on
its color and glowed
like a globe of fire,
and when I wakened
I was alone and the room
still, the white walls,
the white ceiling, the stained
wood floor held me until
I sat up and reached out
first for a glass
of stale water to free
my tongue, and then
the wristwatch purchased
before you were born,
and while the leaves ticked
against the window and
the dust rose golden
in the chalice of the air
I gave you this name.

SPRING IN THE OLD WORLD

In the central terminal rain pouring
through the broken glass on the trains below,
loading and unloading. Above the gray dome
the great sky twisting in from the North Sea.
Cold, wet, wondering, I stood in the corner.
A dark boy walked in off the streets, a shepherd
born of shepherds. At 14 come to Tetuan
for work, then to Ceuta, Algeciras, Amsterdam.
His robes black now with rain, he cracks
sunflower seeds between his teeth, *pipas*
he calls them, and spits the shells and laughs.
In the lower Atlas the hills are green
where his brothers and he raced
through the long grass and wildflowers,
shouting to the air, their skirts
flared out around them, open and burning.

ON THE CORNER

Standing on the corner
until Tatum passed
blind as the sea,
heavy, tottering
on the arm of the young
bass player, and they
both talking
Jackie Robinson.
It was cold, late,
and the Flame Show Bar
was crashing
for the night, even
Johnny Ray
calling it quits.
Tatum said, Can't
believe how fast
he is to first. Wait'll
you see Mays
the bass player said.
Women in white furs
spilled out of the bars
and trickled toward
the parking lot. Now
it could rain, coming
straight down. The man
in the brown hat
never turned his head up.
The gutters swirled
their heavy waters,
the streets reflected
the sky, which was
nothing. Tatum
stamped on toward
the Bland Hotel, a wet
newspaper stuck
to his shoe, his mouth

open, his vest
drawn and darkening.
I can’t hardly wait, he said.

BELLE ISLE, 1949

We stripped in the first warm spring night
and ran down into the Detroit River
to baptize ourselves in the brine
of car parts, dead fish, stolen bicycles,
melted snow. I remember going under
hand in hand with a Polish highschool girl
I'd never seen before, and the cries
our breath made caught at the same time
on the cold, and rising through the layers
of darkness into the final moonless atmosphere
that was this world, the girl breaking
the surface after me and swimming out
on the starless waters towards the lights
of Jefferson Ave. and the stacks
of the old stove factory unwinking.
Turning at last to see no island at all
but a perfect calm dark as far
as there was sight, and then a light
and another riding low out ahead
to bring us home, ore boats maybe, or smokers
walking alone. Back panting
to the gray coarse beach we didn't dare
fall on, the damp piles of clothes,
and dressing side by side in silence
to go back where we came from.

THE FALLING SKY

Last night while I slept
someone woke and went
to the window to see
if the moon was dreaming
in the October night.
I heard her leave the bed,
heard the floor creak
and opened my eyes a moment
to see her standing in all
the glory living gives us.
I caught a scent of lilacs,
and thought, but that was
years ago, and slept again.

Today, I want to ask her
what she hoped to find
last night, I want to say,
I'm with you in this life,
but Nikolai, her boyish
eucalyptus, bucks in the wind,
the long grasses that hold
the seeds of the harvests
to come, give as they must,
and she is busy tying down
and piling dead grass on.

Nothing I can say will stop
the great bellied clouds
riding low over the fences
and flat wooden houses
of this old neighborhood
or keep the late roses
from shredding down to dust.
The first drop splatters
on the back of my hand,
then the second. Time
to go in, says the wind,

and I do. From the window
blurring before my poor eyes,
I see her growing smaller,
darker, under the falling sky.

LET IT BEGIN

Snow before dawn, the trees asleep.
In one window a yellow light—someone
is rising to wash and make coffee
and doze at the table remembering
how a child sleeps late and wakens
drenched in sunlight. If he thinks
of a street, he knows it has gone,
a dog has died, a tulip burned
for an hour and joined the wind.
With the others I drift, useless,
in the parking lot while the day-shift
comes on, or I stand at the corner
as the sun wakens on a gray crust.
The children pass by in silent knots
on the way home from the burial
of the birds. The day has begun.
I can put it away, a white shirt,
unworn, at the back of a drawer,
but my hands are someone else's—
stained, they shine like old wood
and burn in the cold. They have joined
each other in the fellowship
of the shovel. I stood in the temple
of junk where the engine blocks
turned and the nickle-plated grills
dripped on hooks, and though
steel rang on the lip of the furnace
and fire rose out of black earth
and rained down, in the end
I knelt to cinders and ice. I stared
into the needle's dark eye
so the peddler could mend his elbow
and gasp under his sack of rags.
Now the cat pulls on his skullcap
of bones and bows before the mouse.
Light that will spread the morning glory

burns on my tongue and spills
into the small valleys of our living,
the branches creak, and I let it begin.

ANOTHER LIFE

“I’d rather be blind than see this place.”
This place is the prison chapel,
its peeling Last Supper, its portable
plywood confessional. Sunday,
late afternoon, the light going fast
just before the double horn
and the filing to the cells. White haired
black man born in Detroit, my age
almost to the day, his face toothless,
lined, talks about his confinements
as though he’d had four kids, talks
about the poem he can write will follow
me all the way home, try my chair,
eat from my plate, take my voice
until I’m the one walks all night
in the rain, gets stopped by the cops
at dawn, and with the sky reddening
spread my arms and legs against the car
and feel the gloved hand
slide over my balls and pause
and go on, leaving nothing. A day
that begins inside a strange face
swollen and slow,
                                        and ends in the night
with a weak candle, ends as a child,
ends as a gleam of carbon, or gold
blooming from lead, the blue thrill
of wild phlox blooming in the dark
for no one. Ends with Ray Estrada,
his pure face of Andalusia and Indian
gone to fat and scars, telling me
of the farm in Mexico. How he came
at 16 with the waist of a boy to live
here on Trumbull Avenue in the shadow
of the ball park. It’s near dawn
and his grandsons stir in the room
off the kitchen. Outside the rain

has stopped, the streets are quiet at last.
"We don't even have to change for work,"
he says, and raises his bottle
like the trumpets of the Mariachi
and blows into the eye of the wind.

All those years ago, I took up
my breath and walked toward these legs.
Shall I ask why the earth
tires of itself? Shall I ask
how many men, dying, passed me
the blood of their voices, the spittle
oiling their groans. My father's father
hung himself in the hayloft
while the flies circled, and I was born
howling under a tree in Michigan.
That night Harry Levine loaded the car
with samples and headed toward Ohio.
On the road, the moon heard his cries
and when he stopped to vomit
blood and wash his face
in the filling station can, he held
his own head as a mother might
and told himself, "You'll be OK,"
and rinsed his mouth with the gray froth,
went back out under the hidden stars,
paid and turned toward home.
That was one step we took together,
hand in hand. The second was the waking.
Now, before first light, the quail
bark from the orange groves
behind the shed where the day
will find them. Who could have dreamed
these winter orchards where the tree rats
drowse all day, the squirrels
come and go, and one by one the fruit
drops, great sweet navels, rough skinned

and shining, half buried in frosted
winter grass. By noon my woman bows
to the wild brambles and berry bushes,
barren this winter except for the bright
new thorn, green at the shank, red
at the tip, crowned with a globe of blood.

GIFT FOR A BELIEVER

for Flavio Costantini

It is Friday, a usual day
in Italy, and you wait. Below
the street sleeps at noon.
Once the Phoenicians came that way,
the Roman slaves on foot,
and later the Nazis. To you came
the Anarchists chanting, "We shall inherit,"
and among them Santo Caserio
who lost his head for knifing
the President of France, the ambassador
to hell. Came little Ferrer
in his long gown who taught
the Spanish children to question.
His fine hands chained behind
his back, his eyes of a boy
smeared, he swings above the stone trench
of Montjuich. The wind came
to blow his words away, then snow
that buried your childhood
and all the promises, that rusted
out the old streetcars and humped
over your fathers' graves.
In your vision Durruti whispered
to an old woman that he would
never forget the sons and daughters
who died believing they carried
a new world there in their hearts,
but when the doctor was summoned
and could not stop his wounds
he forgot. Ascaso, who fled
with him to Argentina, Paraguay,
Bruxelles, the first to die
storming the Atarazanas Barracks,
he forgot. The railyards of León

where his father doubled over
and deafened, forgotten. That world
that he said is growing here
in my heart this minute
forgotten. When old Nathan Pine
gave two hands to a drop-forge
at Chevy, my spit turned to gall
and I swore I'd never forget.
When the years turned to a gray mist
and my sons grew away without faith,
the memory slept, and I bowed
my head so that I might live.
On the spare hillsides west
of here the new lambs stumble
in the fog and rise. My wife kneels
to the cold earth and we have bread.
I see and don't believe. Farther
west the ocean breaks
on cold stones, the great Pacific
that blesses no one breaks
into water. So this is what
I send you, friend, where you wait
above a street that will waken
into dark shops, sellers of flour
and onions, dogs, hawkers
of salt, iron, lies. I send
water to fill your glass
and overflow, to cool your wrists
in the night ahead, water
that runs like a pure thread
through all my dreams
and empties into tears, water
to wash our eyes, our mothers' last wine,
two palm-fulls the sky gave us,
what the roots crave, rain.

FOR THE POETS OF CHILE

Today I called for you,
my death, like a cup
of creamy milk I
could drink in the cold dawn,
I called you to come
down soon. I woke up
thinking of the thousands
in the *futbol* stadium
of Santiago de Chile,
and I went cold, shaking
my head as though
I could shake it away.
I thought of the men
and women who sang
the songs of their people
for the last time, I
thought of the precise
architecture of a man's wrist
ground down to powder.
That night when I fell asleep
in my study, the false
deaths and the real blurred
in my dreams. I called
out to die, and calling
woke myself to the empty
beer can, the cup
of ashes, my children
gone in their cars,
the radio still moaning.
A year passes, two,
and still someone must
stand at the window
as the night takes hold
remembering how once
there were the voices
of play rising
from the street,

and a man or woman
came home from work
humming a little tune
the way a child does
as he muses over
his lessons. Someone
must remember it over
and over, must bring
it all home and rinse
each crushed cell
in the waters of our lives
the way a god would.
Victor, who died
on the third day—
his song of outrage
unfinished—and was strung
up as an example to all,
Victor left a child,
a little girl
who must waken each day
before her mother
beside her, and dress
herself in the clothes
laid out the night
before. The house sleeps
except for her, the floors
and cupboards cry out
like dreamers. She goes
to the table and sets out
two forks, two spoons, two knives,
white linen napkins gone
gray at the edges,
the bare plates,
and the tall glasses
for the milk they must
drink each morning.

THE SURVIVOR

in memory of my cousin, David Ber Prishkulnick

Nîmes, August, 1966, and I
am going home. Home is here,
you say; your hand reaches
out and touches nothing.
Russia, New York, back,
that was your father; you
took up the road, moving
at dawn or after dusk
in the corrugated Citroen
loaded with shirts and ties.
Light broke in the fields
of poplars and up ahead
was one more village fair
and the peddling.

Once upon a day in 1940
a little man had to leave
his dinner and save his life
and go with his house
on his back, sleeping nowhere,
eating nothing, a shadow
running, a dark stop. That's
how grandpa told the story.
Waking, I found you waiting,
your feet crossed and swinging,
like a child on the bench
outside the window, holding
a sack of warm rolls
for breakfast.

Gray suit, woolen vest,
collar, tie. Now you are
dispersed into the atoms
of gasoline and air

that explode an instant
and are always, dispersed
to the earth that never
warmed you and the rain
drumming down on the hoods
of trucks stalled on the bridge
to Arles. You stop a moment
in my hand that cannot
stop and rise and stumble
onward toward the heart
where there is no rest.

MY SON AND I

In a coffee house at 3 am
and he believes
I'm dying. Outside the wind
moves along the streets
of New York City picking up
abandoned scraps of newspapers
and tiny messages of hope
no one hears. He's dressed
in worn corduroy pants
and shirts over shirts,
and his hands are stained
as mine once were
with glue, ink, paint.
A brown stocking cap
hides the thick blond hair
so unlike mine. For forty
minutes he's tried not
to cry. How are his brothers?
I tell him I don't know,
they have grown away
from me. We are Americans
and never touch on this
stunned earth where a boy
sees his life fly past
through a car window. His mother?
She is deaf and works
in the earth for days, hearing
the dirt pray and guiding
the worm to its feasts. Why
do I have to die? Why
do I have to sit before him
no longer his father, only
a man? Because the given
must be taken, because
we hunger before we eat,
because each small spark
must turn to darkness.

As we said when we were kids
and knew the names of everything
. . . just because. I reach
across the table and take
his left hand in mine.
I have no blessing. I can
tell him how I found
the plum blossom before
I was thirty, how once
in a rooming house in Alicante
a man younger than I,
an Argentine I barely understood,
sat by me through the night
while my boy Teddy cried out
for help, and how when he slept
at last, my friend wept
with thanks in the cold light.
I can tell him that his hand
sweating in mine can raise
the Lord God of Stones,
bring down the Republic of Lies,
and hold a spoon. Instead
I say it's late, and he pays
and leads me back
through the empty streets
to the Earl Hotel, where
the room sours with the mould
of old Bibles dumped down
the air-shaft. In my coat
I stand alone in the dark
waiting for something,
a flash of light, a song,
a remembered sweetness
from all the lives I've lost.
Next door the TV babbles
on and on, and I give up
and sway toward the bed
in a last chant before dawn.

A LATE ANSWER

Beyond that stand of firs
was a small clearing
where the woods ran out
of breath or the winds
beat them back. No one
was born there and no one
would be, but you could
bury a lonely man there
or an animal you didn't
want out for flies to eat.
As we passed under the trees
you were cold and took
my hand and felt a shiver
pass through me, but you
didn't let go. When you
spoke at last it was to ask
after my thoughts, but
just then we broke into light
so unexpected I had to close
my eyes and saw the fire
swimming there and had
such a vision of the end
of my life, the trees
turning to great flowers
of flame and the field ringed
with sword bearing angels.
I could say nothing,
but held on to your hand
and you to mine
both in the dream and in
that bare place where
the North Sea winds lashed
our faces with sudden spurts
of rain. Now, on the other side
of the world, years later,
I know the ant came here
believing he would rule

and he waits for the wren
to fall, the grass waits
blowing its breath
into this morning that rises
darkly on wet winds. Somewhere
the sea saves its tears
for the rising tide, somewhere
we'll leave the world weighing
no more than when we came,
and the answer will be
the same, your hand in mine,
mine in yours, in that clearing
where the angels come toward us
without laughter, without tears.

WAITING

I

Nine years ago, early winter
in Barcelona, the office
of the town doctor. The old
wrapped like the dead, the sick,
the poor, all of us afraid
to be called. In the silence
the sobbing of a civil guard,
his head hung between his knees,
coatless, the leather suspenders
crossed on his back, the holster
shining beside him. His son,
no more then five, cradled
his father's head, stroked
the stubbled cheek from time
to time, and whispering
into his ear pointed
at invisible things
on the smoke-filled air.
The soldier looked up,
he too with the face
of a boy, the eyes brimming,
and said, "I see! I see!"

II

You write from Folsom: "Cold
day, March 20, windy, no one
on the yard." You hear a tv
in the distance, a prison movie
you saw as a teenager in Kansas City,
and beyond that the grating
of steel against rock, you hope,
and maybe voices. You wish
you were guilty, you write,
so you could confess and be pardoned.
Nine years gone down, a wife lost,
and this month a new love gone,

and you'll be 45. "I wish I were
but I'm not so I can't say so."
The judge and the judge's wife
tell me you're where you belong.
No one belongs where you are,
you answer, and you pray for them,
you do, a lot of souls you pray for
down in Fresno. The letter ends,
as always, with a poem, this one
of Ginny, "greener than goose manure
piled five feet high."

III
I look out the window
and the sun rides low in a crown
of mist. Someone is mowing,
the motor starts and stalls and starts
one last time and fades
into the stillness. The calm doctor
who played "futbol" for Barcelona
goes on reading the sports, pulling
at the ends of his moustache,
and we sit in the gold light
of afternoon nine years ago, swimming
in the heavy smoke of tobacco
where everything stays. You sit
at the window above the windswept yard
treeless forever, and you pray
for us all, for the lying witness
left in a ditch, for the stolen car,
for that place you are especially
with its diamond beaten out of clay
and the nine souls who circle the bases
and never score, for the gray walls
the Chinamen made before they starved,
for your own soul, your treasure,
though it thickens like your waist

or like the great oak tree above
your mother's grave. You pray
until the light catches in the branches
of that tree you never saw,
as it does now, and darkens
into sundown and its own life.

ON THE MURDER OF LIEUTENANT JOSÉ DEL CASTILLO BY THE FALANGIST BRAVO MARTÍNEZ, JULY 12, 1936

When the Lieutenant of the Guardia de Asalto
heard the automatic go off, he turned
and took the second shot just above
the sternum, the third tore away
the right shoulder of his uniform,
the fourth perforated his cheek. As he
slid out of his comrade's hold
toward the gray cement of the Ramblas
he lost count and knew only
that he would not die and that the blue sky
smudged with clouds was not heaven
for heaven was nowhere and in his eyes
slowly filling with their own light.
The pigeons that spotted the cold floor
of Barcelona rose as he sank below
the waves of silence crashing
on the far shores of his legs, growing
faint and watery. His hands opened
a last time to receive the benedictions
of automobile exhaust and rain
and the rain of soot. His mouth,
that would never again say "I am afraid,"
closed on nothing. The old grandfather
hawking daisies at his stand pressed
a handkerchief against his lips
and turned his eyes away before they held
the eyes of a gunman. The shepherd dogs
on sale howled in their cages
and turned in circles. There is more
to be said, but by someone who has suffered
and died for his sister the earth
and his brothers the beasts and the trees.

The Lieutenant can hear it, the prayer
that comes on the voices of water, today
or yesterday, from Chicago or Valladolid,
and hangs like smoke above this street
he won't walk as a man ever again.

FOR THE FALLEN

In the old graveyard behind
the fortress of Montjuich
side by side are buried
the brothers Ascaso and
Buenaventura Durruti.
If you go there and stand
in the June sun or under
the scudding clouds
of November you will
hear neither the great wail
of the factories or the sea
groaning into the harbor
laden with goods and freckled
with oil. You will hear
the distant waves of traffic
in the late afternoon rush
and maybe the yellowed grass
eating, for this is that
time in Barcelona, you
will hear your own breath
slowing and time slowing
and then the death of time
because it stops here. You
can go down on your knees
and pray that the spirit
of men and women come back
and inhabit this failing flesh
but if you listen well
your heart will ask
you to stand, under
the fading sun or
the rising moon, it
doesn't matter, either
alone or breathing as you
do now the words
of the fallen and the slow
clouds of diesel exhaust.

Look at your hands. They
are not scarred by
the cigarettes of the police,
and the palms are soft,
the fingers long but
slightly kinked, the hands
once of a boy stained
with the ink of dull reports
the day they laid
Buenaventura beside Francisco
Ascaso and thousands gathered
weeping or somber. The nails
were bitten down then.
The comrades must have known
it was over, and Joaquín
Ascaso, staring at the earth
that had opened so quickly
for his brothers, must
have whispered *soon.*
Soon the boy rose
from his desk and went
into the darkness
congealing in cold parlours
or in the weariness
of old pistons, in the gasps
of men and women asleep
and dreaming as the bus
stalls and starts on the way
home from work. And Joaquín,
who had never knelt, rose
and went home to prepare,
knowing he was all
of them, as you know
they are all that gathers
in your hands, all
that is left, words
spoken to no one

left, blurred in
the waves of the old sea,
garlands of red roses
that tattered, chips
of light and dark, fire
and smoke, the burning
and the cold that were
life and can still
shiver these two stiff
and darkening hands.

ASK THE ROSES

Snow fell forward forever
I heard the trees counting their breaths
the laughter of the icicle
the rivers turning to stone
What became of the sea's dream
to become spirit and range the sky
what became of the astronomy
of the gopher tunneling under the lettuce
and the onion that died like a saint
from the head down
what became of the wooden heart
of the crow who marked our fields
of two codfish end to end
on a blue plate

In the gay parlours of Barcelona
a widow bought an arm and leg
someone else bought all the names
At sea I buy a cloud
and steer it landward into a pile of cars
I buy a mountain oak
and feed it cocaine until the leaves gag
I read the wolf the oath of office
until he sheds his coat, bites
off his forepaws and howls
for the grave
In front of everyone
I take out my money and count it
stacking the 50's, the 20's, and the 10's
The House of Peace, The Mansion of Wisdom,
The Tenement of Beauty
and the Martial Arts, Survival and Torture
We drink to the health of the dollar
Let my people go, say the coins
herded into the black purse
and headed for Germany
No one is going anywhere

we've all come into our own
and we're staying

There are tall reedy weeds by the fence
the fallen oranges in my neighbor's yard
blacken and spread like shotgun wounds
Down south in L.A. they are pouring
milk back to the sewers
Has anyone asked the cows
has anyone told the sunset
it will be on tv or the child
that her breasts filled with plastic
will sell fried chicken
Has anyone told the sea it must count
its tears and explain each one
has anyone told the blood
how long it must crust the sheets
had anyone asked the roses
if they love bees who are
basically communists
and worship the female
has anyone fallen on his knees
and begged the dawn to reconsider
Perhaps it is too late, now
with the golden light of Tarragona
darkening into lead I want to take
a vow of silence, every word
is a young mouse growing in my throat
stretching his paws
trying out his pink nails
As light enters the morning glory
I feel the heart of a tree swell
and grow into mine, as light falls
through the tunnels of branches
that lead back the way I came
I rise from this grave and go
My aunt and my mother sit again

as in the first dreams of home
crying with love for each other
exchanging words they will forget
Later there will be silence
houses will die around them
My aunt will waken in a motel
outside Fort Dix without a name
In the movies my mother will see
the future and run weeping
along the black staircases
studded with huge breathless stars
The old sun will darken like the spots
on her hands, the light will pass early
and she will go on wiping at the air
as at a window, wondering, Is it there
All around her Los Angeles goes on
moaning and blooming, and I wait
for the bus that never comes
or punch the time-card
after the clock has stopped

Let the leaves falling singly in my hair
get up and join the tree
let the unread books open
into the nests of barn swallows
or turn to twigs and long grass
yellowing in the summer winds
Let the smell of the egg
mate with the rose and the voice
of elm cry out at dusk, a cat
who will no longer hunt
calling for food, my old cat
full of foolishness and hungers
Shall we dye her blue, call her
"California" and teach her how to turn
how to walk on stage, how to hold
the mouse in her paws

Every evening we show her television
blackening the screen when the lions
drink in the crowded stream

The pen that told the truth melted
on the stove, the ink that held
in its veins the bones
of the eel, let go
They became dirt
metals that are earth and can't fly
or must return to spring water
bitter in a tin cup
A man shelling peas sleeps
under the quarter moon
Anyone who laughs out of turn
must eat flies
At dusk no one dares
if a woman passed me now
she would yell at her dog
snap the leash and try to look old
If she cast her eyes to the ground
I would smell it and shake her head
until her hair caught fire
Smelling myself I think of old clothes
schoolrooms the rain entered and killed
of a leather purse lost at sea
of a mule bleeding along the whipped flanks
a wind passing through a burned hand
the black embers flaking
of air a dog wouldn't breathe
I am space alone, unfilled, waiting day
after day for two people to be together
or only one who could sigh and be still

AND THE TRAINS GO ON

We stood at the back door
of the shop in the night air
while a line of box cars
of soured wheat and pop bottles
uncoupled and was sent creaking
down our spur. Once, when I
unsealed a car and the two
of us strained the door open
with a groan of rust, an old man
stepped out and tipped his hat.
'It's all yours, boys!'
and he went off, stiff-legged,
smelling of straw and shit.
I often wonder whose father
he was and how long he kept
moving until the police
found him, ticketless, sleeping
in a 2nd class waiting room
and tore the cardboard box
out of his hands and beat him
until the ink of his birth smudged
and surrendered its separate vowels.
In the great railyard of Milano
the dog with the white throat
and the soiled muzzle crossed
and recrossed the tracks
"searching for his master,"
said the boy, but his grandfather
said, "No. He was sent by God
to test the Italian railroads."
When I lie down at last to sleep
inside a boxcar of coffins bound
for the villages climbing north
will I waken in a small station
where women have come to claim
what is left of glory? Or will
I sleep until the silver bridge

spanning the Mystic River jabs
me awake, and I am back
in a dirty work-shirt that says *Phil,*
24 years old, hungry and lost, on
the run from a war no one can win?
I want to travel one more time
with the wind whipping in
the open door, with you to keep
me company, back the long
tangled road that leads us home.
Through Flat Rock going east
picking up speed, the damp fields
asleep in moonlight. You stand
beside me, breathing the cold
in silence. When you grip
my arm hard and lean way out
and shout out the holy names
of the lost neither of us is scared
and out tears mean nothing.

TO MY GOD IN HIS SICKNESS

I

A boy is as old as the stars
that will not answer
as old as the last snows
that blacken his hands
though he wakes at 3
and goes to the window
where the crooked fence is blessed
and the long Packard
and the bicycle wheel
though he walk the streets
warm in the halo of his breath
and is blessed over and over
he will waken in the slow dawn
he will call his uncles out
from the sad bars of Irish statesmen
all the old secret reds
who pledged in the park
and raise drinks
and remember Spain

Though he honor the tree
the sierra of snow
the stream that died years ago
though he honor his breakfast
the water in his glass
the bear in his belly
though he honor all crawling
and winged things
the man in his glory
the woman in her salt
though he savor the cup of filth
though he savor Lake Erie
savor the rain burning down
on Gary, Detroit, Wheeling
though my grandmother argues
the first cause of night

and the kitchen cantor mumbles his names
still the grave will sleep

I came this way before
my road ran by your house
crowded with elbows of mist
and pots banging to be filled
my coat was the colors of rain
and six gray sparrows sang
on the branches of my grave

II
A rabbit snared in a fence of pain
screams and screams
I waken, a child again
and answer
I answer my father
hauling his stone up the last few breaths
I answer Moses bumbling before you
the cat circling three times
before she stretches out and yawns
the mole gagged on fresh leaves

In Folsom, Jaroubi, alone before dawn
remembers the long legs of a boy
his own once and now his son's
Billy Ray holds my hand to his heart
in the black and white still photograph
of the exercise yard
in the long shadows of the rifle towers
we say goodbye forever
Later, at dusk the hills
across the dry riverbed
hold the last light
long after it's gone
and glow like breath

I wake
and it's not a dream
I see the long coast of the continent
writhing in sleep
this America we thought we dreamed
falling away flake by flake
into the sea
and the sea blackening and burning

I see a man curled up, the size of an egg
I see a woman hidden in a carburetor
a child reduced to one word
crushed under an airmail stamp
or a cigarette

Can the hands rebuild the rocks
can the tongue make air or water
can the blood flow back
into the twigs of the child
can the clouds take back their deaths

III
First light of morning
it is the world again
the domed hills across the gorge
take the air slowly
the day will be hot and long
Jimmy Ray, Gordon, Jaroubi
all the prisoners have been awake
for hours remembering
I walk through the dense brush
down to the river
that descended all night from snow
small stones worn away
old words, lost truths
ground to their essential nonsense
I lift you in my hand

and inhale, the odor of light
out of darkness, substance out of air
of blood before it reddens and runs

When I first knew you
I was a friend to the ox and walked
with Absalom and raised my hand
against my hand
and died for want of you
and turned to stone and air and water
the answer to my father's tears

A NOTE ABOUT THE AUTHOR

Philip Levine was born in 1928 in Detroit and was formally educated there, at the public schools and at Wayne University (now Wayne State University). After a succession of industrial jobs he left the city for good and lived in various parts of the country before settling in Fresno, California, where he taught at the University until his retirement. He has received many awards for his books of poems, most recently the National Book Award in 1991 for *What Work Is,* and the Pulitzer Prize in 1995 for *The Simple Truth.*

A NOTE ON THE TYPE

The text of this book is set in a typeface named Plantin, a digitized version of a metal design cut in 1913 by The Monotype Corporation of London. Though the face bears the name of Christopher Plantin of Antwerp, who in the latter part of the sixteenth century owned the largest printing and publishing firm in Europe, it is a free adaptation of designs by Claude Garamond (c. 1480–1561) made for that firm. With its strong, simple lines, Plantin is a face of exceptional legibility.

Composition by NK Graphics, Keene, New Hampshire
Printed and bound by Quebecor Printing, Fairfield, Pennsylvania
Designed by Harry Ford